Collins

Grammar, Punctuation and Vocabulary Progress Tests

Year 1 / P2

Author:
Sarah Snashall

Series editor:
Stephanie Austwick

William Collins' dream of knowledge for all began with the publication of his first book in 1819. A self-educated mill worker, he not only enriched millions of lives, but also founded a flourishing publishing house. Today, staying true to this spirit, Collins books are packed with inspiration, innovation and practical expertise. They place you at the centre of a world of possibility and give you exactly what you need to explore it.

Collins. Freedom to teach.

Published by Collins
An imprint of HarperCollins*Publishers*
The News Building
1 London Bridge Street
London SE1 9GF

Browse the complete Collins catalogue at www.collins.co.uk

© HarperCollins*Publishers* Limited 2019

10 9 8 7 6 5 4 3 2 1

ISBN 978-0-00-833360-7

All rights reserved. No part of this publication may be reproduced, stored in a retrieval system, or transmitted in any form by any means, electronic, mechanical, photocopying, recording or otherwise, without the prior written permission of the Publisher or a licence permitting restricted copying in the United Kingdom issued by the Copyright Licensing Agency Ltd., Barnard's Inn, 86 Fetter Lane, London, EC4A 1EN.

British Library Cataloguing in Publication Data. A catalogue record for this publication is available from the British Library.

Author: Sarah Snashall

Series Editor: Stephanie Austwick

Publisher: Katie Sergeant

Product Manager: Sarah Thomas

Content Editor: Holly Woolnough

Copyeditor and proofreader: Tanya Solomons

Reviewer: Rachel Clarke

Internal design and typesetting: Hugh Hillyard-Parker

Cover designers: The Big Mountain Design and Ken Vail Graphic Design

Illustrations: Sue Woollatt from Graham-Cameron Illustration and Jouve India Private Limited

Production Controller: Katharine Willard

Contents

How to use this book ... 4

Year 1 Curriculum Map: Yearly overview ... 6

Year 1/P2 Half Termly Tests
Autumn Half Term 1 ... 7
Autumn Half Term 2 ... 13
Spring Half Term 1 ... 19
Spring Half Term 2 ... 25
Summer Half Term 1 ... 31
Summer Half Term 2 ... 38

Mark schemes
Autumn Half Term 1 ... 46
Autumn Half Term 2 ... 47
Spring Half Term 1 ... 48
Spring Half Term 2 ... 49
Summer Half Term 1 ... 50
Summer Half Term 2 ... 51

Record sheet ... 53

How to use this book

Introduction

Collins *Grammar, Punctuation and Vocabulary Progress Tests* have been designed to give you a consistent whole-school approach to teaching and assessing grammar, punctuation and vocabulary. Each photocopiable book covers the required vocabulary, grammar and punctuation objectives from the English National Curriculum statutory guidance and vocabulary, grammar and punctuation appendix. For teachers in Scotland, the books can offer guidance and structure that is not provided in the Curriculum for Excellence Experiences and Outcomes or Benchmarks.

Revision of previous years' work is also included, where appropriate, to ensure children are building their skills to become confident and secure users of grammar, punctuation and vocabulary. As standalone tests, independent of any teaching and learning scheme, the Collins *Grammar, Punctuation and Vocabulary Progress Tests* provide a structured way to assess progress in grammar, punctuation and vocabulary, to help you identify areas for development, and to provide evidence towards expectations for each year group.

Building confidence and understanding

At the end of Key Stage 1 and Key Stage 2, children are assessed on their understanding of grammar, punctuation and vocabulary. This is done through teacher assessment of children's writing, through the grammar, punctuation and vocabulary SAT in KS2 and through the optional SAT in KS1. Collins *Grammar, Punctuation and Vocabulary Progress Tests* have been designed to help children recognise grammatical features whilst building familiarity with the format, language and style of the SATs. Through regular use of the Collins *Grammar, Punctuation and Vocabulary Progress Tests* children should develop and practise the necessary skills to complete the national tests confidently and proficiently.

The Collins *Grammar, Punctuation and Vocabulary Progress Tests* are written so that new grammatical content is presented in a variety of ways with increasing challenge over the tests in the book. Previous learning is also addressed in Years 2 – 6 with questions that ask children to recall grammar, punctuation and vocabulary learned in previous year groups.

How to use this book

In this book, you will find six photocopiable half-termly tests, written to replicate the format of the SATs with space for children to write their answers. You will also find a Curriculum Map on page 6 indicating the aspects of the Content Domain covered in each test and across the year group. These have been cross-referenced with the appropriate age-related statements from the National Curriculum. In KS2, each test should take 35 – 45 minutes to complete and in KS1 each test should take approximately 20 minutes. KS1 teachers may prefer to administer each test in two halves of 10 minutes each, and in Year 1 read each question to children.

To help you mark the tests, you will find mark schemes that include the number of marks to be awarded, model answers and a reference to the elements of the Content Domain covered by each question.

Test demand

The tests have been written to ensure smooth progression in children's understanding of grammar, punctuation and vocabulary within the book and across the rest of the books in the series. Each test builds on those before it so that children are guided towards the expectations of the SATs at the end of KS1 and KS2.

Year 1: How to use this book

Year group	Number of marks per test
1	20
2	20
3	30
4	30
5	40
6	50

Performance thresholds

The table below provides guidance for assessing how children perform in the tests. Most children should achieve scores at or above the expected standard with some children working at greater depth and exceeding expectations for their year group. Whilst these threshold bands do not represent standardised scores, as in the end of key stage SATs, they will give an indication of how children are performing against the expected standard for their year group.

Year group	Working towards	Expected standard	Greater depth
1	9 marks or below	10–16 marks	17–20 marks
2	9 marks or below	10–16 marks	17–20 marks
3	14 marks or below	15–25 marks	26–30 marks
4	14 marks or below	15–25 marks	26–30 marks
5	18 marks or below	19–33 marks	34–40 marks
6	23 marks or below	24–42 marks	43–50 marks

Tracking progress

A record sheet is provided to help you illustrate to children the areas in which they have performed well and where they need to develop. A spreadsheet tracker is also provided via **collins.co.uk/assessment/downloads** which enables you to identify whole-class patterns of attainment. This can then be used to inform your next teaching and learning steps.

Editable download

All the files are available in Word and PDF format for you to edit if you wish. Go to **collins.co.uk/assessment/downloads** to find instructions on how to download. The files are password protected and the password clue is included on the website. You will need to use the clue to locate the password in your book. You can use these editable files to help you meet the specific needs of your class, whether that be by increasing or decreasing the challenge, by reducing the number of questions, by providing more space for answers or increasing the size of text as required for specific children.

© HarperCollinsPublishers Ltd 2019

Year 1 Curriculum map: Yearly overview

National Curriculum objective (Year 1)	Content domain	Autumn Test 1	Autumn Test 2	Spring Test 1	Spring Test 2	Summer Test 1	Summer Test 2
WORD							
Regular plural noun suffixes [-s; es], including the effects of these suffixes on the meaning of the noun	G6	●					●
Suffixes that can be added to verbs where no change is needed in the spelling of root words [for example, helping, helped, helper]	G6	●	●		●	●	●
How the prefix un- changes the meaning of verbs and adjectives [for example, untie: untie the boat]	G6		●		●		●
SENTENCE							
Combine words to make sentences	G2 G3	●	●	●	●	●	●
Joining words and joining clauses using and	G3		●	●	●	●	●
PUNCTUATION							
Separation of words with spaces	G3	●	●	●	●	●	●
Capital letters and full stops to demarcate sentences	G5	●	●	●	●	●	●
Question marks to demarcate sentences	G2 G5				●	●	●
Exclamation marks to demarcate sentences	G2 G5	●	●	●	●	●	●
Capital letters for names of people	G5			●	●	●	●
Capital letters for names of places	G5			●		●	
Capital letters for days of the week	G5		●	●	●	●	
Capital letters for the personal pronoun I	G5	●	●	●	●	●	●

Content Domain Key
G1: Grammatical terms / word clauses
G2: Functions of sentences
G3: Combining words, phrases and clauses
G4: Verb tenses and consistency
G5: Punctuation
G6: Vocabulary

Name: Year: Date:

Autumn Half Term 1

1 Circle the **full stop** in this sentence.

That is a big hat.

1 mark

2 Circle the **capital letter** in this sentence.

This is a fat rat.

1 mark

3 Tick the word that ends with <u>ing</u>.

✓ Tick **one**.

dressing ☐

dressed ☐

1 mark

4 Match the words with the same ending.

Draw **two** lines.

| jumping | • | • | helped |
| jumped | • | • | helping |

1 mark

5 Tick the word that needs a **capital letter**.

✓ Tick **one** box.

put it in the box.

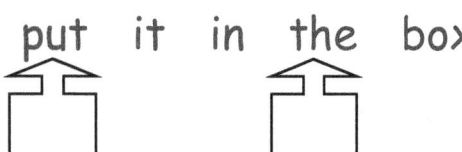

6 Draw a line to the word that is written correctly.

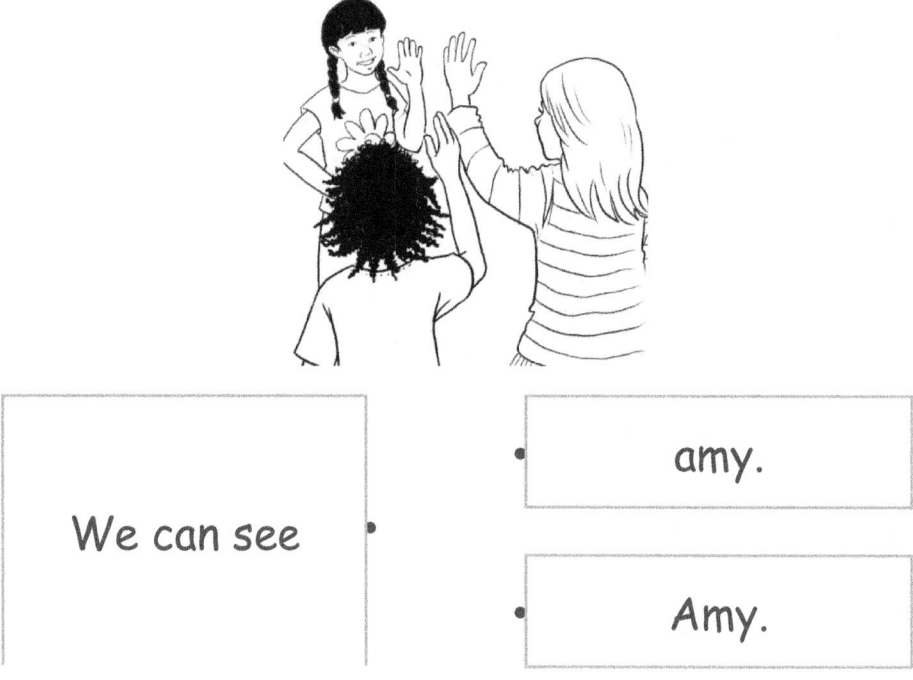

We can see — amy.

— Amy.

7 Circle the correct words.

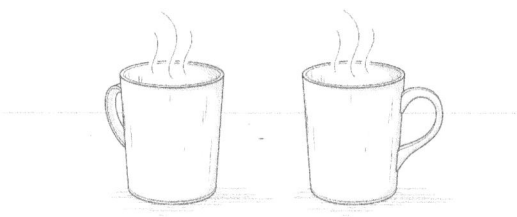

two mug   two mugs

8 Circle the correct words.

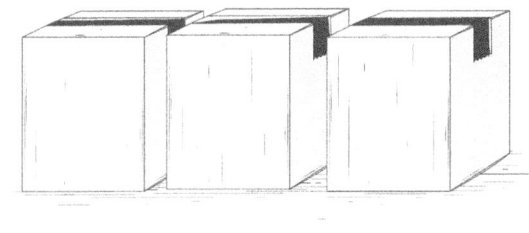

three box   three boxes

1 mark

9 Circle **one** word that needs a **capital letter**.

Dad   and   i   like   to   swim.

1 mark

10 Circle the word that ends with <u>ed</u>.

Dad   sorted   out   my   room.

1 mark

11 Circle the correct sentence.

Hinata is sleep.   Hinata is sleeping.

1 mark

12 Which of these are spelled correctly?

✓ Tick **two**.

one wish, two wishs ☐

one wish, two wishes ☐

one lap, two laps ☐

one lap, two lapes ☐

13 Tick the word that is a **noun**.

✓ Tick **one** box.

Dan　has　ten　books.

14 Write the sentence correctly.

Here comes jim.

_____

15 Add <u>ing</u> to the word <u>clean</u> to make the sentence correct.

Gok is clean_____ his teeth.

16 Add <u>er</u> or <u>ed</u> to the word <u>want</u> to make the sentence correct.

Sam wanted a cat but Kim want_____ a puppy.

17 Tick the word that is a **verb**.

✓ Tick **one** box.

The zebra runs fast.

18 Write the missing word.

one dress   two _____

19 Write a sentence about the picture.

_____

_____

2 marks

Total: _____ /20 marks

Autumn Half Term 2

1 Which is correct?

✓ Tick **one**.

This is a bag ☐

This is a bag. ☐

1 mark

2 Draw a line to the correct punctuation to end the sentence.

1 mark

3 Tick the word that needs a **capital letter**.

✓ Tick **one** box.

can we go to the park?
⇑   ⇑
☐   ☐

1 mark

4 Draw a line to the word that is written correctly.

1 mark

5 Match the words with the same ending.

Draw **three** lines.

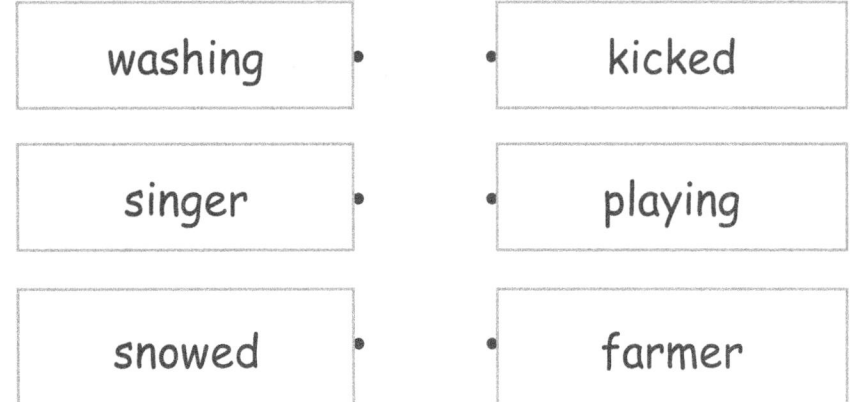

1 mark

6 Match the words that are opposites.

Draw **three** lines.

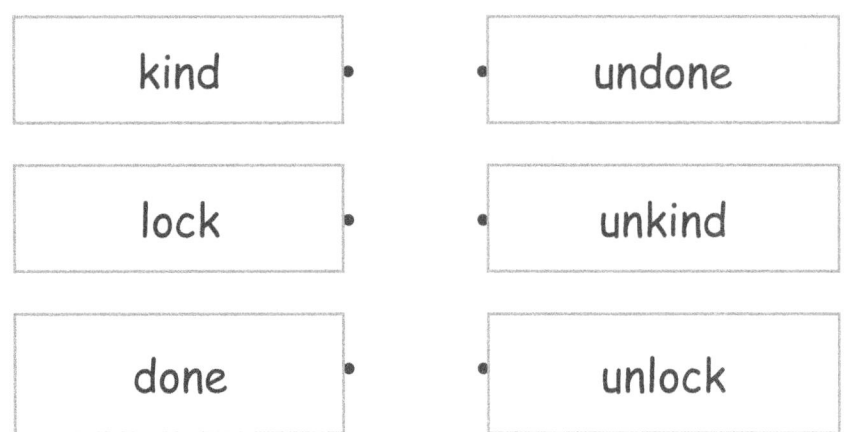

1 mark

7 Which is correct?

✓ Tick **one**.

where is Ada. ☐

Where is Ada ☐

Where is Ada? ☐

1 mark

8 Circle the word that means <u>not lucky</u>.

The   bird   sees   the   unlucky   snail.

1 mark

9 Circle **one** word that needs a **capital letter** in the sentence below.

Mum   and   i   like   to   eat   cake.

1 mark

10 Add <u>ing</u> to the word <u>play</u> to make the sentence correct.

Jim is play_____ football with Josh.

1 mark

11 Tick the word that is a **verb**.

✓ Tick **one** box.

The girls skip in the playground.
⬆   ⬆

1 mark

12 Why does the word A<u>jit</u> have a **capital letter** in the sentence below?

My brother A<u>jit</u> is very clever.

✓ Tick **one**.

It is an important word. ☐
It is a person's name. ☐
It is the first word in the sentence. ☐
It is a mistake. ☐

1 mark

13 Tick the word that is a **noun**.

✓ Tick **one** box.

We hope to go to the beach.
     ⬆   ⬆

1 mark

14 Write the sentence correctly.

This is Mrs ali.

_____

1 mark

15 Write the sentence correctly.

Josh and i talk too much.

_____

1 mark

16 Add <u>un</u> to the word <u>tidy</u> to make a word that means <u>not tidy</u>. Write the word.

_____

1 mark

17 Tick the correct word to complete the sentence below.

I am _____ for my book.

✓ Tick **one**.

look ☐

looked ☐

looking ☐

1 mark

18 Use the words below to write a sentence about the picture. Remember to use correct punctuation.

boy   the   sand   digging   is   the   in

_____

1 mark

19 Write a sentence the girl in the picture could say.

2 marks

Total: _____ /20 marks

Spring Half Term 1

1 Circle the **question mark** in the sentence below.

Can you see my sister ?

1 mark

2 Which is correct?

✓ Tick **one**.

Lola has lost her gloves ☐

lola has lost her gloves ☐

Lola has lost her gloves. ☐

1 mark

3 Tick the word in the sentence below that needs a **capital letter**.

✓ Tick **one** box.

I live in york.

1 mark

4 Tick the words that need a **capital letter**.

✓ Tick **two** boxes.

Can bel and i join your game?

1 mark

Year 1: Spring Half Term Test 1

5 Circle the correct sentence.

Kim has two bag.

Kim has two bags.

1 mark

6 Circle the correct sentence.

The foxs are in the bush.

The foxes are in the bush.

1 mark

7 Tick the word that is a **verb**.

✓ Tick **one** box.

The mouse hides in the cupboard.

1 mark

8 Tick the correct word to complete the sentence below.

Zack has the car _____ Bill has the truck.

✓ Tick **one**.

the	☐
and	☐
on	☐
which	☐

1 mark

9 Which is correct?

✓ Tick **one**.

Do you want a drink?	☐
do you want a drink.	☐
Do you want a drink.	☐

1 mark

10 Tick the name of the punctuation mark that should complete each sentence.

Sentence	Full stop	Question mark
This is my bag		
Where is your bag		

1 mark

11 Circle the correct sentence.

I helped Dad dry the dishes.

I helped Dad dry the dishs.

1 mark

12 Write the sentence correctly.

We are going to london.

_____

1 mark

13 Why does the word <u>Scotland</u> have a **capital letter** in the sentence below?

Edinburgh is the capital of Scotland.

✓ Tick **one**.

It is the most important word. ☐

It is a person's name. ☐

It is the name of a place. ☐

It is a mistake. ☐

1 mark

14 Write the missing word.

one frog   two _____

1 mark

15 Write the missing word to complete the sentence.

Pedro has one bunch of bananas.

Pedro has two _____ of bananas.

1 mark

16 Sally can sing. Sally can dance.

Which option correctly combines these two sentences with <u>and</u>?

✓ Tick **one**.

Sally can sing. And Sally can dance. ☐

Sally can sing and dance. ☐

Sally can sing. and can dance. ☐

Sally can sing. ☐

1 mark

17 Write these sentences as one sentence.

Ruben is going shopping. Ronnie is going shopping.

_____

1 mark

18 Use the words below to write a **question**. Remember to use correct punctuation.

pen   I   your   borrow   can

_____

1 mark

19 Write a **question** the boy on the left could ask.

_____
_____

2 marks

Total: _____ /20 marks

Spring Half Term 2

1 Circle the **exclamation mark** in the sentence below.

The old man was kind!

1 mark

2 Draw a line to the correct punctuation to end the sentence.

1 mark

3 Circle the word in the sentence below that needs a **capital letter**.

We will do PE on tuesday.

1 mark

4 Tick the words that need a **capital letter**.

✓ Tick **two** boxes.

1 mark

5 Tick the word that is a **verb**.

✓ Tick **one** box.

I hear loud drums.
 ⇧   ⇧
 ☐   ☐

1 mark

6 Add ed or er to the word wait to complete the sentence.

We wait_____ a long time for the bus.

1 mark

7 Circle the correct sentence.

It is my birthday on monday.

It is my birthday on Monday.

1 mark

8 Tick the words that need a **capital letter**.

✓ Tick **three**.

wednesday ☐

i ☐

lemon ☐

liam ☐

1 mark

9 Tick the name of the punctuation mark that should complete each sentence.

Sentence	Exclamation mark	Question mark
Watch out		
What is your name		
Help me		
How are you feeling		

1 mark

10 Tick the correct word to complete the sentence below.

Jun went home _____ ate his dinner.

✓ Tick **one**.

and ☐

who ☐

my ☐

the ☐

1 mark

11 Circle the correct sentence.

Pablo unwraps the present he has been given.

Pablo wraps the present he has been given.

1 mark

12 The cat has soft fur. The cat has a long tail.

Which option correctly combines these two sentences with <u>and</u>?

✓ Tick **one**.

The cat has soft fur and a long tail. ☐

The cat has soft fur. ☐

Cats have soft fur and long tails. ☐

The cat has soft and long fur. ☐

1 mark

13 Match each word to its meaning.

Draw **three** lines.

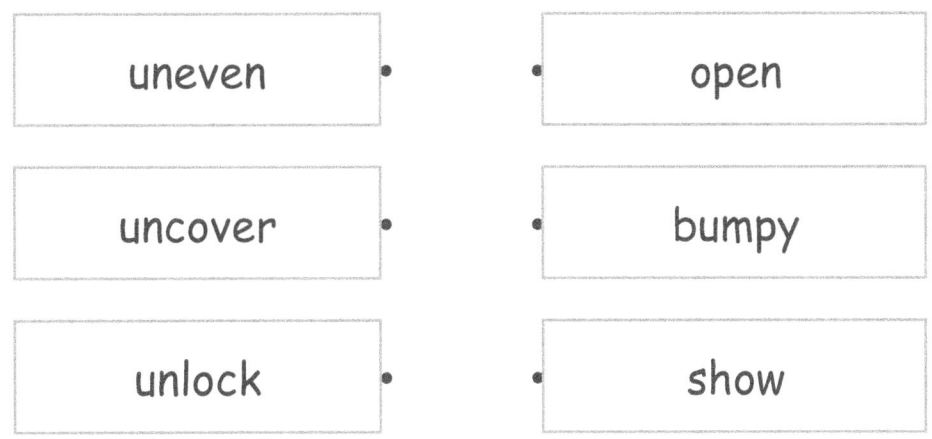

1 mark

14 Add <u>un</u> to the word <u>do</u> to make a new word.
Write the word to complete the sentence.

I must _____ my shoelaces.

1 mark

15 Write these sentences as one sentence.

Zain is funny. Zain is kind.

_____

1 mark

16 Write these sentences as one sentence.

Zosia bakes a cake. Fergus washes up.

_____

1 mark

17 How do the letters <u>un</u> change the word <u>fold</u>?

fold → **unfold**

✓ Tick **one**.

They put it into the past tense. ☐

They make it a plural. ☐

They make it into a noun. ☐

They turn it into an opposite. ☐

1 mark

18 Use the words below to write a **question**. Remember to use correct punctuation.

you   and   Tish   Can   Saturday   on   come

_____

1 mark

19 Write an **exclamation** the girl on the right could shout.

2 marks

Total: _____ /20 marks

Summer Half Term 1

1 What type of punctuation mark is used at the end of these sentences?

We have to run! The bus is coming!

✓ Tick **one**.

question mark	☐
exclamation mark	☐
full stop	☐

1 mark

2 Match each sentence to the correct punctuation mark.

Draw **three** lines.

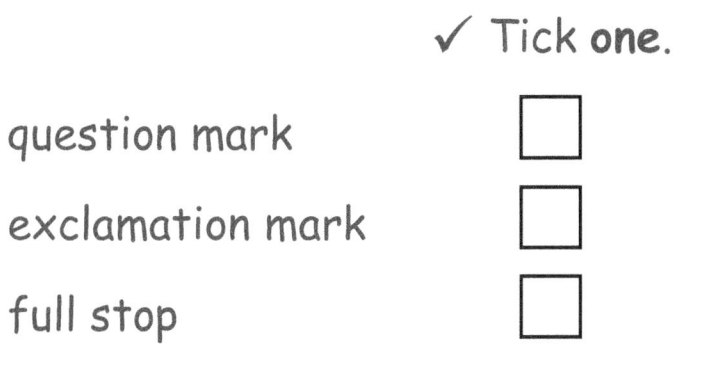

1 mark

Year 1: Summer Half Term Test 1

3 Tick the word in the sentence below that needs a **capital letter**.

✓ Tick **one** box.

Mum said i could go swimming.

1 mark

4 Tick the word in the sentence below that needs a **capital letter**.

✓ Tick **one** box.

I saw six fluffy chicks at packford Farm.

1 mark

5 Which sentence is punctuated correctly?

✓ Tick **one**.

Lily found the missing coin ☐

Lily found the missing coin. ☐

lily found the missing coin ☐

Lily found the missing coin? ☐

1 mark

6 Circle the correct sentence.

I drank three glasses of squash!

I drank three glasss of squash!

1 mark

7 Tick the word that is a **verb**.

✓ Tick **one** box.

The hero saves the little girl.

1 mark

8 Match each word to the correct option.

Draw **two** lines.

| push + ing | • | • | pushhing |

• pushing

| read + ing | • | • | reading |

• readding

1 mark

9 Add <u>ed</u> or <u>er</u> to the word <u>play</u> to make a word that means <u>someone who plays</u>.

We needed one more play____ to join our game.

1 mark

10 Jackson is seven. Anya is five.

Which option correctly combines these two sentences into one sentence?

✓ Tick **one**.

Jackson and Anya are seven.	☐
Jackson is seven.	☐
Jackson is seven Anya is five.	☐
Jackson is seven and Anya is five.	☐

1 mark

11 Are these words spelled correctly or incorrectly? Tick **one** box in each row.

Word	Correct	Incorrect
otters		
paintes		
wishes		
pushs		

1 mark

12 Why does the word <u>Fatima</u> have a capital letter in the sentence below?

Mrs Jones asked Fatima to clean the board.

✓ Tick **one**.

She is doing the cleaning.	☐
To make you say it loudly.	☐
It is someone's name.	☐
It is one of the days of the week.	☐

1 mark

13 Tick the correct word to complete the sentence below.

Mr Dirty hated _____ his hair.

✓ Tick **one**.

washing	☐
washed	☐
washer	☐
washes	☐

1 mark

14 Add <u>ed</u>, <u>er</u> or <u>ing</u> to the end of the word <u>brush</u> to correct the sentence.

Jeela pulled up her socks and <u>brush</u> her hair.

1 mark

15 Which ending is needed to make each word plural? Tick **one** box in each row.

Word	Add s	Add es
one bike, two bike__		
one watch, two watch__		
one brush, two brush__		
one banana, two banana__		

1 mark

16 Use <u>and</u> to write these two sentences as one sentence.

I have put on a jumper. I have put on a hat.

_____

_____

1 mark

17 Can the sentences be joined to make one sentence by using <u>and</u>? Tick **one** box in each row.

Sentence	Yes	No
The cat is black. Let's go out.		
My chair is too low. I can't reach the table.		

1 mark

18 Use the words below to write a **question**.
Remember to use correct punctuation.

match   tomorrow   a   there   football   is

_____

1 mark

19 Write a **question** the boy could ask the girl.

2 marks

Total: _____ /20 marks

Summer Half Term 2

1 Match each punctuation mark to its name.

Draw **three** lines.

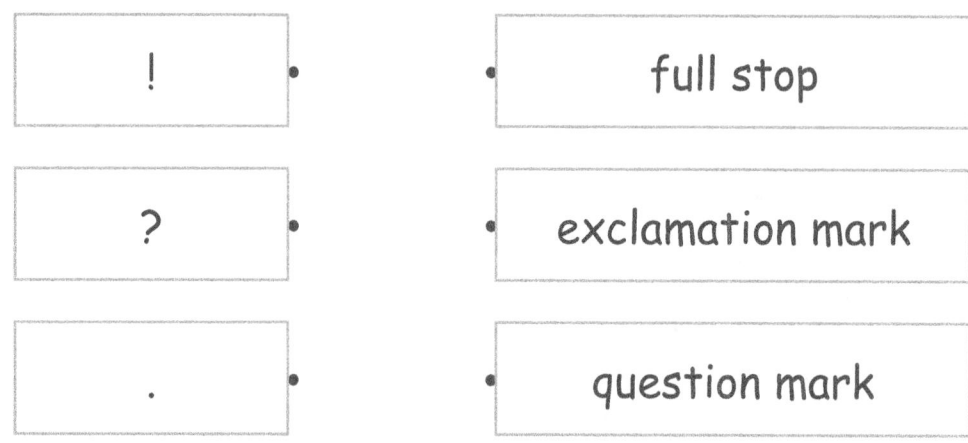

1 mark

2 Which sentence is punctuated correctly?

✓ Tick **one**.

the school will be closed on Friday. ☐

The school will be closed on friday. ☐

The school will be closed on Friday. ☐

The school will be closed on Friday ☐

1 mark

3 Tick the word in the sentence below that needs a **capital letter**.

✓ Tick **one** box.

We found a funny card for martha.
    ⇧   ⇧   ⇧
    ☐   ☐   ☐

1 mark

4 Tick the word that is a **noun**.

✓ Tick **one** box.

I have lost my hat.
         ⇧   ⇧
         ☐   ☐

1 mark

5 Tick the name of the punctuation mark that should complete each sentence.

Sentence	Exclamation mark	Question mark
What shall we give Eva		
What a mess		
What time will they arrive		
What a lovely picture that is		

1 mark

6 Match each word to its meaning.

Draw **four** lines.

1 mark

7 Tick the ending needed to complete the word.

	Add ing	Add ed
Stop push___!		
We have pass___ my house.		
It snow___ yesterday.		
Are you go___ to the party?		

1 mark

8 Match each sentence to its missing word.

Draw **three** lines.

You are _____ hard! •	• worker
You have _____ hard! •	• working
You are a hard _____! •	• worked

1 mark

9 Tick the best word to complete the sentence below.

Please help me to _____ the shopping.

✓ Tick **one**.

unhappy ☐
undo ☐
unpack ☐
unfold ☐

1 mark

10 Which option is punctuated correctly?

✓ Tick **one**.

The house was old. It frightened Max. ☐

The house was old it frightened Max ☐

The house was old it frightened Max. ☐

the house was old. it frightened Max. ☐

1 mark

11 Circle the **two** words in this sentence that need a **capital letter**.

Next   week   poppy   and   i   will   swap   places.

1 mark

12 Rewrite the underlined words to correct the sentence.

Mr Nabil put <u>five bag and two box</u> in his van.

[   ]

1 mark

13 Which option uses the word <u>and</u> correctly.

✓ Tick **one**.

The hamster runs and into the corner hides. ☐

The hamster runs into the corner. and the hamster hides. ☐

The hamster runs into the corner and hides. ☐

And the hamster runs. And into the corner hides. ☐

1 mark

14 Circle the **two** words in this sentence that need a **capital letter**.

Our class is going to leeds on friday.

1 mark

15 Add <u>ed</u>, <u>er</u> or <u>ing</u> to the end of the word <u>splash</u> to correct the sentence. Write the word.

Look at how the ducks are <u>splash</u> in the water!

☐

1 mark

16 Use <u>and</u> to write these two sentences as one sentence.

I will visit Kobe on Saturday. I will play computer games with him.

_____

_____

1 mark

17 Can the sentences be joined to make one sentence by using <u>and</u>? Tick **one** box in each row.

Sentence	Yes	No
It's raining. The washing is getting wet.		
I will put on my hat. I will put on my gloves.		
The pie is hot. It is Saturday.		

1 mark

18 Rewrite the sentence below correctly. Remember to use correct punctuation.

dad will go to italy on monday

_____

1 mark

19 Write an **exclamation** the mother could be saying to the girl.

Remember to use correct punctuation.

2 marks

Total: _____ /20 marks

Year 1: Autumn Half Term Test 1 - Mark Scheme

Mark scheme for Autumn Half Term 1

Qu.	Requirement	Mark
1 G5	**Award 1 mark** for the full stop circled.	1m
2 G5	**Award 1 mark** for the capital letter of *This* circled. **Also award the mark** if the whole of the word *This* is circled.	1m
3 G6	**Award 1 mark** for the box next to *dressing* ticked. **Also award the mark** for the word *dressing* ticked.	1m
4 G6	**Award 1 mark** for both lines drawn correctly: jumping = helping jumped = helped	1m
5 G5	**Award 1 mark** for a tick in the box under *put*. **Also award the mark** for the word *Put* written out and spelled correctly, with a capital letter.	1m
6 G5	**Award 1 mark** for the line drawn correctly: We can see = Amy.	1m
7 G6	**Award 1 mark** for *two mugs* circled. **Also award the mark** for the words *two mugs* written out and spelled correctly.	1m
8 G6	**Award 1 mark** for *three boxes* circled. **Also award the mark** for the words *three boxes* written out and spelled correctly.	1m
9 G5	**Award 1 mark** for the word *i* circled.	1m
10 G6	**Award 1 mark** for the word *sorted* circled.	1m
11 G6	**Award 1 mark** for the sentence *Hinata is sleeping.* circled.	1m
12 G6	**Award 1 mark** for the second and third boxes ticked correctly: one wish, two wishes one lap, two laps	1m
13 G1	**Award 1 mark** for a tick in the box under *books*. **Also award the mark** for the word *books* ticked.	1m
14 G5	**Award 1 mark** for the sentence *Here comes Jim.* written with capital letters for *Here* and *Jim*, a full stop at the end and spaces between the words.	1m
15 G6	**Award 1 mark** for the letters *ing* written on the line. **Also award the mark** for the word *cleaning* written out and spelled correctly.	1m
16 G6	**Award 1 mark** for the letters *ed* written on the line. **Also award the mark** for the word *wanted* written out and spelled correctly.	1m
17 G1	**Award 1 mark** for a tick in the box under *runs*. **Also award the mark** for the word *runs* ticked.	1m
18 G6	**Award 1 mark** for the word *dresses* written out and spelled correctly.	1m
19 G3	**Award 1 mark** for a sentence that matches the brief with spaces between the words. **Award 1 mark** for a capital letter and a full stop used correctly. (Total 2 marks)	2m

Mark scheme for Autumn Half Term 2

Qu.	Requirement	Mark
1 G5	**Award 1 mark** for the box next to *This is a bag.* ticked. **Also award the mark** for the sentence *This is a bag.* circled.	1m
2 G5	**Award 1 mark** for the line drawn correctly: What is the time = ?	1m
3 G5	**Award 1 mark** for a tick in the box under *can*. **Also award the mark** for the word *Can* written out and spelled correctly, with a capital letter.	1m
4 G5	**Award 1 mark** for the line drawn correctly: Let us help = Jack.	1m
5 G6	**Award 1 mark** for all three lines drawn correctly: washing = playing singer = farmer snowed = kicked	1m
6 G6	**Award 1 mark** for all three lines drawn correctly: kind = unkind lock = unlock done = undone	1m
7 G5	**Award 1 mark** for a tick in the box next to *Where is Ada?*	1m
8 G6	**Award 1 mark** for the word *unlucky* circled.	1m
9 G5	**Award 1 mark** for the word *i* circled.	1m
10 G6	**Award 1 mark** for the letters *ing* added to the word *play*.	1m
11 G1	**Award 1 mark** for a tick in the box under *skip*.	1m
12 G5	**Award 1 mark** for a tick in the box next to *It is a person's name.*	1m
13 G1	**Award 1 mark** for a tick in the box under *beach*.	1m
14 G5	**Award 1 mark** for the sentence *This is Mrs Ali.* written with capital letters for *This, Mrs* and *Ali*, a full stop at the end and spaces between the words.	1m
15 G5	**Award 1 mark** for the sentence *Josh and I talk too much.* written with capital letters for *Josh* and *I*, a full stop at the end and spaces between the words.	1m
16 G6	**Award 1 mark** for the word *untidy* spelled correctly.	1m
17 G6	**Award 1 mark** for a tick in the box next to *looking*.	1m
18 G3	**Award 1 mark** for the sentence *The boy is digging in the sand.* spelled correctly and punctuated with a capital letter and a full stop, and spaces between the words. **Also award the mark** for any sentence that matches the picture and has a capital letter, a full stop and spaces between the words.	1m
19 G3	**Award 1 mark** for a sentence that matches the brief with spaces between the words. **Award 1 mark** for a capital letter and a full stop used correctly. (Total 2 marks)	2m

Year 1: Spring Half Term Test 1 – Mark scheme

Mark scheme for Spring Half Term 1

Qu.	Requirement	Mark
1 G5	**Award 1 mark** for the question mark circled.	1m
2 G5	**Award 1 mark** for a tick in the box next to *Lola has lost her gloves.* **Also award the mark** for *Lola has lost her gloves.* circled.	1m
3 G5	**Award 1 mark** for a tick in the box under *york*. **Also award the mark** for *york* circled or the word *York* written correctly.	1m
4 G5	**Award 1 mark** for ticks in the boxes under *i* and *bel*. **Also award the mark** for both *i* and *bel* circled.	1m
5 G6	**Award 1 mark** for the sentence *Kim has two bags.* circled.	1m
6 G6	**Award 1 mark** for the sentence *The foxes are in the bush.* circled.	1m
7 G1	**Award 1 mark** for a tick in the box under *hides*.	1m
8 G3	**Award 1 mark** for the word *and* ticked.	1m
9 G5	**Award 1 mark** for the sentence *Do you want a drink?* ticked.	1m
10 G5	**Award 1 mark** for both answers ticked correctly: This is my bag = Full stop Where is your bag = Question mark	1m
11 G6	**Award 1 mark** for the sentence *I helped Dad dry the dishes.* circled.	1m
12 G5	**Award 1 mark** for the sentence *We are going to London.* written with capital letters for *We* and *London*, a full stop at the end and spaces between the words.	1m
13 G5	**Award 1 mark** for a tick in the box next to *It is the name of a place.* **Also award the mark** for the sentence *It is the name of a place.* circled.	1m
14 G6	**Award 1 mark** for the word *frogs* spelled correctly.	1m
15 G6	**Award 1 mark** for the word *bunches* spelled correctly.	1m
16 G3	**Award 1 mark** for a tick in the box next to *Sally can sing and dance.* **Also award the mark** for the sentence *Sally can sing and dance.* circled.	1m
17 G3	**Award 1 mark** for the sentence *Ruben and Ronnie are going shopping.* if it is spelled and punctuated correctly. **Also award the mark** for *Ruben is going shopping and Ronnie is going shopping.* if it is spelled and punctuated correctly.	1m
18 G3	**Award 1 mark** for the question *Can I borrow your pen?* spelled correctly and punctuated with a capital letter and a question mark, and spaces between the words.	1m
19 G3	**Award 1 mark** for a question that matches the brief with spaces between the words. **Award 1 mark** for a capital letter and a question mark used correctly. (Total 2 marks)	2m

Mark scheme for Spring Half Term 2

Qu.	Requirement	Mark
1 G5	**Award 1 mark** for the exclamation mark circled.	1m
2 G5	**Award 1 mark** for the line drawn correctly: What is your name = ?	1m
3 G5	**Award 1 mark** for the word *tuesday* circled. **Also award the mark** for the word *Tuesday* written correctly.	1m
4 G5	**Award 1 mark** for ticks in the boxes under *mia* and *i*. **Also award the mark** for the words *mia* and *i* circled.	1m
5 G1	**Award 1 mark** for a tick in the box under *hear*.	1m
6 G6	**Award 1 mark** for the letters *ed* added to the word *wait*.	1m
7 G5	**Award 1 mark** for the sentence *It is my birthday on Monday.* circled.	1m
8 G5	**Award 1 mark** for ticks in the boxes next to *wednesday*, *i* and *liam*. **Also award the mark** for the correct words circled.	1m
9 G5	**Award 1 mark** for three or four correct answers: Watch out = Exclamation mark What is your name = Question mark Help me = Exclamation mark How are you feeling = Question mark	1m
10 G3	**Award 1 mark** for a tick in the box next to *and*. **Also award the mark** for the word *and* circled.	1m
11 G6	**Award 1 mark** for the sentence *Pablo unwraps the present he has been given.* circled.	1m
12 G3	**Award 1 mark** for a tick in the box next to *The cat has soft fur and a long tail.*	1m
13 G6	**Award 1 mark** for all three lines drawn correctly: uneven = bumpy uncover = show unlock = open	1m
14 G6	**Award 1 mark** for the word *undo* spelled correctly and written on the line.	1m
15 G3	**Award 1 mark** for a sentence that correctly uses *and* and is punctuated correctly, for example: *Zain is funny and kind.* or *Zain is funny and Zain is kind.* or *Zain is funny and he is kind.*	1m
16 G3	**Award 1 mark** for the sentence *Zosia bakes a cake and Fergus washes up.* if it is spelled and punctuated correctly.	1m
17 G6	**Award 1 mark** for a tick in the box next to *They turn it into an opposite.*	1m
18 G3	**Award 1 mark** for the question *Can you and Tish come on Saturday?* spelled correctly and punctuated with capital letters for *Saturday* and *Can*, and a question mark.	1m
19 G3	**Award 1 mark** for a sentence that matches the brief with spaces between the words. **Award 1 mark** for a capital letter and an exclamation mark used correctly. (Total 2 marks)	2m

Year 1: Summer Half Term Test 1 – Mark scheme

Mark scheme for Summer Half Term 1

Qu.	Requirement	Mark
1 G5	**Award 1 mark** for a tick in the box next to exclamation mark.	1m
2 G5	**Award 1 mark** for all three lines drawn correctly: Let's go = ! Which one do you want = ? I have a pet hamster = .	1m
3 G5	**Award 1 mark** for a tick in the box under *i*. **Also award the mark** for the word *i* circled.	1m
4 G5	**Award 1 mark** for a tick in the box under *packford*.	1m
5 G5	**Award 1 mark** for a tick in the box next to *Lily found the missing coin*.	1m
6 G6	**Award 1 mark** for the sentence *'I drank three glasses of squash!'* circled. **Also award the mark** for just the word *glasses* circled.	1m
7 G1	**Award 1 mark** for a tick in the box under *saves*.	1m
8 G6	**Award 1 mark** for both lines drawn correctly: push + ing = pushing read + ing = reading	1m
9 G6	**Award 1 mark** for the letters *er* added to the word *play*.	1m
10 G3	**Award 1 mark** for a tick in the box next to *Jackson is seven and Anya is five*.	1m
11 G6	**Award 1 mark** for three or four correct answers: otters = Correct paintes = Incorrect wishes = Correct pushs = Incorrect	1m
12 G5	**Award 1 mark** for a tick in the box next to *It is someone's name*.	1m
13 G6	**Award 1 mark** for a tick in the box next to *washing*.	1m
14 G6	**Award 1 mark** for the word *brushed* written in the box.	1m
15 G6	**Award 1 mark** for three or four correct answers: one bike, two bike = Add s one watch, two watch = Add es one brush, two brush = Add es one banana, two banana = Add s	1m
16 G3	**Award 1 mark** for the sentence *I have put on a jumper and a hat.* if it is spelled and punctuated correctly. **Also award the mark** for *I have put on a jumper and I have put on a hat.* or *I have put on a jumper and hat.*	1m
17 G3	**Award 1 mark** for both answers correct: The cat is black. Let's go out. = No My chair is too low. I can't reach the table. = Yes	1m
18 G3	**Award 1 mark** for the question *Is there a football match tomorrow?* spelled correctly and punctuated with a capital letter and a question mark, and spaces between the words.	1m
19 G3	**Award 1 mark** for a sentence that matches the brief with spaces between the words. **Award 1 mark** for a capital letter and a question mark used correctly. (Total 2 marks)	2m

Mark scheme for Summer Half Term 2

Qu.	Requirement	Mark
1 G5	**Award 1 mark** for all three lines drawn correctly: ! = exclamation mark ? = question mark . = full stop	1m
2 G5	**Award 1 mark** for a tick in the box next to *The school will be closed on Friday.*	1m
3 G5	**Award 1 mark** for a tick in the box under *martha*. **Also award the mark** for the word *Martha* written correctly next to the word.	1m
4 G1	**Award 1 mark** for a tick in the box under *hat*.	1m
5 G5	**Award 1 mark** for three or four correct answers: What shall we give Eva = Question mark What a mess = Exclamation mark What time will they arrive = Question mark What a lovely picture that is = Exclamation mark	1m
6 G6	**Award 1 mark** for all four lines drawn correctly: unblock = stop something being blocked unhappy = not happy undress = take clothes off uncover = take a cover off	1m
7 G6	**Award 1 mark** for three or four correct answers: Stop push____! = Add ing We have pass___ my house. = Add ed It snow___ yesterday. = Add ed Are you go___ to the party? = Add ing	1m
8 G6	**Award 1 mark** for all three lines drawn correctly: You are _____ hard! = working You have _____ hard! = worked You are a hard _____! = worker	1m
9 G6	**Award 1 mark** for a tick in the box next to *unpack*.	1m
10 G5	**Award 1 mark** for a tick in the box next to *The house was old. It frightened Max.*	1m
11 G5	**Award 1 mark** for the words *poppy* and *i* circled.	1m
12 G6	**Award 1 mark** for the phrase *five bags and two boxes* written in the box correctly.	1m
13 G3	**Award 1 mark** for a tick in the box next to *The hamster runs into the corner and hides.*	1m
14 G5	**Award 1 mark** for the words *leeds* and *friday* circled.	1m
15 G6	**Award 1 mark** for the word *splashing* written in the box.	1m
16 G3	**Award 1 mark** for the sentence *I will visit Kobe on Saturday and play computer games with him.* **Also award the mark** for *I will visit Kobe on Saturday and we will play computer games.* or *I will visit Kobe on Saturday and I will play computer games with him.*	1m

Year 1: Summer Half Term Test 2 – Mark scheme

17 G3	**Award 1 mark** for two or three correct answers: It's raining. The washing is getting wet. = Yes. I will put on my hat. I will put on my gloves. = Yes The pie is hot. It is Saturday. = No	1m
18 G3	**Award 1 mark** for the sentence *Dad will go to Italy on Monday.* written correctly with spaces between the words, capital letters for *Dad*, *Italy* and *Monday*, and a full stop.	1m
19 G3	**Award 1 mark** for a sentence that matches the brief with spaces between the words. **Award 1 mark** for a capital letter and an exclamation mark used correctly. (Total 2 marks)	2m

Name: Class:

Year 1 Grammar, Punctuation and Vocabulary Record Sheet

Tests	Mark	Total marks	Key skills to target
Autumn Half Term Test 1			
Autumn Half Term Test 2			
Spring Half Term Test 1			
Spring Half Term Test 2			
Summer Half Term Test 1			
Summer Half Term Test 2			

www.ingramcontent.com/pod-product-compliance
Lightning Source LLC
Chambersburg PA
CBHW081419300426
44109CB00019BA/2352